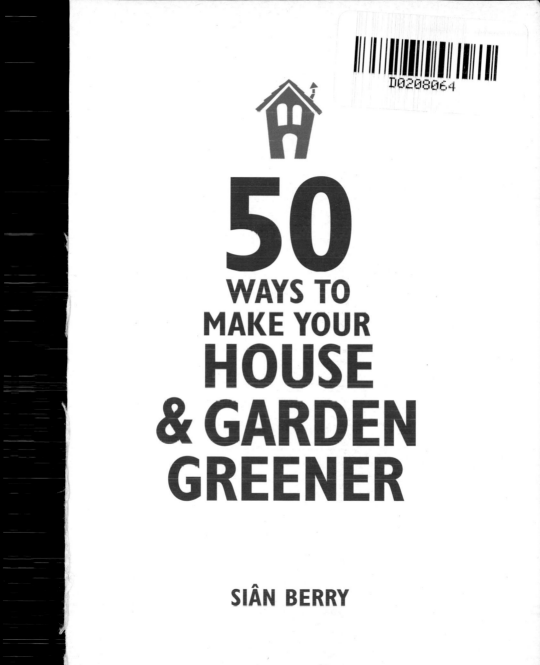

50

WAYS TO
MAKE YOUR
HOUSE
& GARDEN
GREENER

SIÂN BERRY

ABOUT THE AUTHOR

Siân Berry is the Green Party's candidate for London Mayor in 2008 and is a founder of the successful campaign group, the Alliance Against Urban 4x4s.

Siân was one of the Green Party's Principal Speakers until September 2007 and was previously national Campaigns Co-ordinator. She stood in the Hampstead and Highgate constituency in the 2005 General Election and has campaigned in her local area for more affordable housing and, nationally, to promote renewable energy and local shops.

Famous for the mock parking tickets created by Siân in 2003, the Alliance Against Urban 4x4s is now a national campaign and the group recently celebrated persuading the current Mayor of London to propose a higher congestion charge for big 4x4 vehicles and other gas-guzzlers.

Siân studied engineering at university and her professional background is in communications. These skills give her a straightforward and accessible approach to promoting green issues, focusing on what people can do today to make a difference, and on what governments need to do to make greener lives easier for everyone.

As spokesperson for the Alliance and a well-known Green Party figure, Siân has received wide coverage in national and international newspapers and has appeared on numerous TV and radio shows, from Radio 4's *Today* programme to *Richard and Judy*. Her calm, cheerful and persuasive advocacy has stimulated a lively public debate about 4x4s, and has helped to raise the environment further up the public agenda.

50
WAYS TO
MAKE YOUR
HOUSE
& GARDEN
GREENER

SIÂN BERRY

Kyle Cathie Ltd

First published in Great Britain in 2007 by
Kyle Cathie Ltd
122 Arlington Road, London NW1 7HP
general.enquiries@kyle-cathie.com
www.kylecathie.com

10 9 8 7 6 5 4 3 2 1

978-1-85626-722-4

Editorial Director: Muna Reyal
Illustrator and Designer: Aaron Blecha
Production Director: Sha Huxtable
Junior Editor: Danielle Di Michiel

A Cataloguing In Publication record for this title is
available from the British Library.

Colour reproduction by Scanhouse
Printed and bound in Italy by Amadeus

Printed on 100% recycled paper

WHAT'S THE USE OF A FINE HOUSE IF YOU HAVEN'T GOT A TOLERABLE PLANET TO PUT IT ON?

Henry David Thoreau

50 WAYS...

In the home, in the garden, at the shops, at work and on the move, this series of books contains a wide range of simple ways to live a greener life, whatever your situation. Each book has 50 easy, affordable and creative tips to help you live more lightly on the planet.

There are many ways to be green that don't need a big investment of money, time, effort or space. Saving energy also saves money on your bills, and eco-friendly products don't have to be high-tech or expensive.

Any size garden – or even a window box – can be a haven for wildlife and provide useful low-maintenance crops that save on imported fruit and vegetables. And those of us living in towns and cities should know that urban living can provide some of the lowest-carbon lifestyles around.

The *50 ways* series has been written by Siân Berry: Green Party candidate for Mayor of London in 2008 and a founder of the successful campaign group, the Alliance Against Urban 4x4s. She shares her experiences to demonstrate how you can reduce your carbon footprint, stay ahead of fashion and enjoy life without sacrifice.

Siân says, 'Being green is not about giving everything up; it's about using things cleverly and creatively to cut out waste. In these books, I aim to show you that a greener life without fuss is available to everyone.'

INTRODUCTION

As a member of the Green Party, I am working to make big changes to the way our society is run. My aim is to make the greenest options the easiest and cheapest options for everyone.

But people don't want to wait; they want to help reduce climate change and improve their environment now. The advice they get from newspapers and television is often contradictory and confusing, and people are crying out for information they can trust.

I am often asked by friends, colleagues and people on the street for tips on how to be green. So, in this book, I have collected together 50 of the most useful things you can do in your house and garden today to have a positive impact on the planet.

This book is not a shopping list of shiny new things to buy; neither is it a sermon, full of things you have to give up. In fact, I hope it will give you lots of good ideas for new and interesting things to try.

Follow the tips you can, and don't feel guilty about those you can't. Where green living meets a barrier is where we need campaigners and politicians to step in and remove it, so do get in touch (or even start a campaign of your own) if your eco-friendly efforts hit problems.

In picking my favourite house and garden tips for this book, I have focused on things which have the biggest impact, which are fun and easy to do, and which bring other benefits with them. Many of these tips will save you time and money – making saving the planet a bonus.

BEING GREENER IN THE HOUSE

The vast majority of energy used in the home, adding to the cost of our bills and our carbon footprint, is for heating and cooling our living spaces. More than four fifths of the gas and electricity we use goes on this one job.

In reducing our impact on the planet, keeping ourselves warm while using less energy is the most important action we can take, so that's why the chapter on heating and cooling is the first one in this section.

But lots of smaller actions make a difference, too. Much of the energy consumed by our daily lives is simply wasted rather than doing a useful job. These bits of needless waste are often easily solved, and every single one helps in reducing our carbon footprint.

If you could see carbon dioxide emissions, they might look a bit like litter in the park. There are big eyesores you can point to, such as that abandoned shopping trolley, but every little bit of rubbish is part of the problem, contributing to making the place look a mess.

Reducing the carbon footprint of your home is a bit like clearing up this litter, although, of course, it is a lot more fun! You might need help to deal with the biggest energy-wasting 'eyesores', but energy goes to waste around the home in lots of little ways as well, and these are all worth dealing with.

HEATING AND COOLING

Keeping our homes warm in winter and cool in summer creates a large proportion of our carbon emissions, but there are some very simple ways to make savings using both natural and high-tech methods.

One of the pioneers of energy saving, Amory Lovins, the founder of the Rocky Mountain Institute in the USA, built one of the most heat-efficient houses in the world in the 1980s.

The walls of his home are well insulated, with 40cm cavity walls filled with foam and another 20–30cm of foam on the roof. His windows are double-glazed with heat-reflecting film, and heat is recovered from the ventilation system, so even in the biting Colorado winter, he doesn't need to use any artificial means of heating.

Dr Lovins says that he can make up the 100 watt total heat loss of his house, 'by playing with my dog, who generates about 50 watts of heat, adjustable to 100 watts if you throw a ball to her'.

Having no energy bills is appealing, but even if you can't build a state-of-the-art eco-home from scratch, there's a lot you can do with a draughty old house or flat to reduce your carbon footprint – and save pots of cash in the process. After all, saving energy is a lot cheaper than buying it.

1 INSULATE

The energy efficiency of new homes varies enormously around the world. Colder countries, such as Sweden, have the highest levels of insulation, but in temperate areas, such as the UK, building standards are some of the worst in the world.

British homes currently lose around half their heat through their roofs and walls, so dramatic savings can come from improved insulation.

Loft insulation can save a third of heating costs. Simply filling cavity walls can reduce heat loss by 60 per cent, and it's so cheap to install you can make your money back within a year or two.

Solid walls, with no cavity, are much more expensive to deal with, as material must be attached to the outside of the house, or panels fitted to the inside of exterior walls.

However, it makes even more of a difference to your bills, so look out for grants and special offers from local and national government and from energy companies to help cover the cost of insulation.

Deal with Draughty Windows and Doors

These can be the weak points in the insulation of any house. In old homes, more than a fifth of heat loss can be due to draughts, so a simple roll of draught excluder can be a really cheap and easy way to cut your losses. Don't forget the letter box, which can bring a blast of cold air into your hallway if it doesn't have an insulating brush.

Why not hang a curtain in front of an exterior door for extra insulation? A heavy fabric can give a medieval feel to a hallway, and a funky pattern can add drama to your kitchen. Regardless of climate considerations, it will look much nicer than a plain door.

Another 20 per cent of heat can be lost through single-glazed windows. Double-glazing can reduce heat losses by more than half and is now available not just in ugly white PVC, but with wooden frames to fit all kinds of windows.

For some reason, many radiators (including mine) are placed under windows, letting a lot of their heat straight out through the draughts and gaps. If the people who built your house put radiators by the window too, avoid hanging long curtains in front to make this worse.

13

2 TURN DOWN THE THERMOSTAT

It's easy to leave your thermostat at too high a setting. You come in on a cold day with frozen hands, and you want to warm up quickly, so you knock the dial up a degree or two and then leave it on the same setting for days.

Turning down the heating is almost always the first point in any energy-saving checklist. That's because it's easy, instant and saves you money. So, here's that famous fact again: turning down your thermostat by one degree can save you 10 per cent on your heating bill.

Twenty degrees is plenty for a comfortable room temperature – if you're moving around, even less than this is fine. If you're sitting down to watch TV for the evening, snuggle in properly with a blanket or throw, rather than getting up to adjust the heat when you feel chilly.

Try my extra tip of turning the heating right down when you leave the house. My cat doesn't seem to mind this at all.

And don't forget the water heating. If your boiler has a thermostat, 60°C is ample to provide hot showers and washing-up.

SOLAR HEATING 3

You don't need fancy panels on your roof to use the power of the sun to heat your home.

Even in winter, sunlight streaming through windows can make several degrees of difference to the temperature. Why else would tender plants survive the cold months in a greenhouse?

New homes are being built with this in mind, with larger windows on south-facing walls and a reduced number of smaller windows to the north.

You can get the maximum benefit of the sun by opening curtains on south- or east-facing windows as soon as you get up in the morning. This will raise the temperature naturally and reduce the work your heating system needs to do.

4 SOLAR WATER HEATING

Solar hot-water systems are one of the best-value ways of using solar energy in the home. The panels on the roof don't generate electricity but instead capture the heat from the sun and transfer it to a water tank through a heat exchanger.

They are very common now in hot countries. If you have been on holiday to the Mediterranean recently, you may have experienced solar water heating in action. Holiday apartments often have these systems installed. But, even in less sunny areas, they can still save you a huge amount of energy. There are twenty-one million homes in the UK alone that have the potential to use solar heating.

A well-designed system can last for twenty years, and can really help to reduce your energy bills, providing up to 2,000kWh of energy a year – enough for half the hot water needs of a family of four.

If you want to use solar energy but not spend a fortune, solar water heating is one of the best new technologies to invest in. As with other kinds of renewable energy, there are often grants available to help with the cost.

NO-POWER COOLING 5

As climate change makes extremes of temperature more common, air-conditioning is gaining popularity. But shutting all the doors and relying on an energy-hungry refrigeration unit to stay comfortable isn't the only answer. Just by opening doors and windows strategically around the house, you can very effectively ventilate your home and keep the temperature down.

Open windows both upstairs and downstairs, and as hot air escapes from the top of the house, it will pull air into the bottom and set up an effective cooling cycle.

If you live in a flat or single-storey house, you can still use your windows to exploit this effect. Many kinds of windows can be opened to create a gap at the top and bottom of the window frame. Engineers have modelled air flow and worked out that this is a good way of cooling a room.

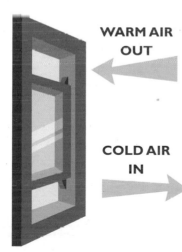

WARM AIR OUT

COLD AIR IN

By creating roughly equal gaps, a cycle is created, with warm air flowing out at the top and pulling cooler air in below.

Leaving windows in this position overnight is even better, as this will cool the walls and the rest of the room, which can then absorb heat throughout the following day. Try it, and see what a difference it makes before investing money in fans and air-conditioning!

SAVING ELECTRICITY

John Lennon could have said, 'There's nothing you can do that can't be done... while also using up electricity'. I recently visited my sister and asked if I could get a glass of water. I was sent to a water cooler and found that, not only was this machine using electricity to cool the water, I also had to press a button so that electricity could pump the water in a thin stream into my glass – which took ages. OK, it was very cold water, but what's wrong with a tap?

Many electronic machines are designed to be left constantly on standby, waiting for our attention. Some of these are so badly designed they use up nearly the same amount of electricity on standby as when they are on full power.

More and more of our gadgets also need charging up from the mains and these adaptors, particularly those for mobile phones, are often left constantly powered up.

Although the efficiency of major household appliances has improved steadily, the electricity consumption of appliances in the average household has more than doubled in the last thirty years, because we now have so many more things that need plugging in.

This doesn't have to continue if we use electricity more efficiently. And this doesn't mean not having useful gadgets; just reducing the electricity we waste on doing non-useful things. Being more aware of the electricity we waste can save us all money on our bills as well as cut down on the climate damage done by all those power stations.

6 FREE YOURSELF FROM GADGETS

Household surveys have shown that, compared with the 1970s, the number of different kinds of electrical gadgets in the typical home has increased from seventeen to thirty seven.

Some of the new machines I have in my home do exciting things I wouldn't want to give up, such as provide Wi-Fi access or play DVDs. But many people stop using gadgets after only a few tries, and every year many electrical gadgets given as Christmas presents are never used at all.

Things such as washing machines are genuinely labour saving. But many appliances are simply more trouble than they are worth. With only a tiny bit of practice, it's much quicker to use a knife to shred a cabbage than it is to get out the multi-purpose food mixer, plug it in, find the right attachments and then feed the vegetables through the tube.

Food mixers have been on the consumer durable shopping list for years, but a more recent trend is for mini-bar-style small fridges. Research has shown that most of these are only kept full for a short novelty period. After that, many are left switched on for months with virtually nothing inside, adding to people's electricity bills while cooling nothing more than thin air.

Say no to needless gadgets and you'll save time, trouble and attic space!

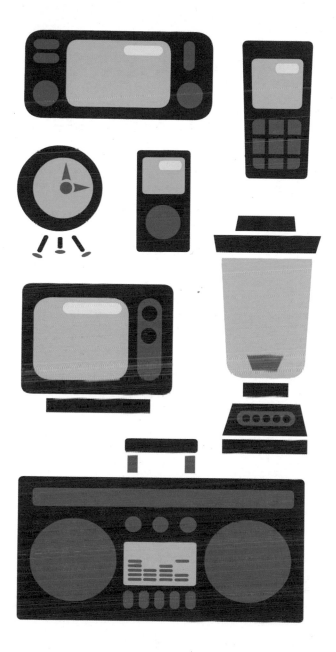

7 BE ENERGY-AWARE

The chart below shows the electricity consumed by different kinds of electrical goods around the home.

Electronic goods are the fastest-growing user of electricity and are soon expected to overtake the current heaviest users: cold appliances, such as fridges and freezers.

Appliances in the kitchen are responsible for almost half the electricity footprint of a home, and saving energy in the kitchen is covered in the next chapter.

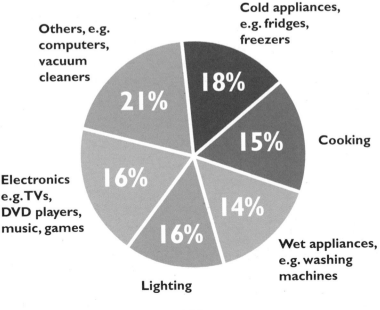

Cold appliances, e.g. fridges, freezers

Others, e.g. computers, vacuum cleaners

21%

18%

15% Cooking

Electronics e.g. TVs, DVD players, music, games

16%

16%

14%

Wet appliances, e.g. washing machines

Lighting

Choose your appliances wisely

When shopping for large household appliances, you can find out a lot about their energy consumption before you buy. Many shops have large energy-rating certificates displayed, and this is helping more of us to choose the best A-rated products.

Be careful if you are getting a new television. Energy ratings aren't always shown on these items, but the cost of running large new models can be considerable. A plasma-screen television can cost twice as much to run as the traditional set it replaces and, despite the growth in all the other kinds of electronic machines, by 2020 about half the energy consumed by electronics in the home will be powering televisions.

But saving energy isn't just about getting the most energy-efficient appliances. How these products are used also makes a big difference.

Watch your meter in action

One gadget I do recommend is a device that talks remotely to your electricity meter to give you a portable readout of the electricity your home is consuming. You can set it to show the energy, cost or carbon emissions of your electricity supply.

With one of these, saving energy becomes a real adventure, as you can walk around the house and check the impact on the reading when you turn on different pieces of equipment. It can also save you a lot of money.

When people get solar panels, they also get a 'smart meter' like this to show the power they are generating. Not counting the energy from the solar panels, people use up to 25 per cent less electricity with one of these meters installed, simply because they are more aware of when they are wasting it.

8 VAMPIRE ELECTRONICS

The problem of standby power consumption is getting a lot of attention, but it's amazing how many products still come without a proper off switch.

Although the standby power of each item is usually low, the total cost to our energy bills and the environment is high. The USA needs an extra twelve power stations thanks to the electricity being sucked out of the grid by machines on standby.

The worst culprits are still consumer electronics such as TV sets, VCRs and games consoles. Considering they are such recent innovations, it's odd to find out that games machines are some of the most wasteful things. If not shut down, these machines remain in 'idle' mode, consuming virtually all the power used in 'on' mode. It's as if someone is playing a game twenty-four hours a day, and even an addicted teenager would find it hard to manage that.

There's one simple answer to all of this: getting into the habit of turning things off at the plug is the best way of making sure you don't contribute to the standby problem.

Try to get extension leads which have individual switches for each plug, so you can turn off individual items rather than leave everything else on standby because you need one of the sockets.

And look for appliances which have low standby power consumption. This is usually shown on the box, so aim for standby consumption of 1W or less.

Unplug that charger

Cordless gadgets that need charging up
with an external adaptor are increasing
rapidly – more than a billion new chargers
are produced worldwide every year.

On the one hand this could be good
for the environment, as rechargeable
machines are replacing those that used
to rely on toxic batteries. But many
chargers, particularly those for mobile phones,
are left plugged in, where they continue to
use up power all the time.

You can feel how much just by touching them.
Adaptors give off a considerable amount of heat as
they convert mains electricity to the charging voltage,
even when they are not charging up a device.

A very easy habit to break is that of charging your
mobile phone overnight. Only an hour or two of
charging, at most, is enough for most phones, so the
power used during the rest of the night is all wasted.
Plugging in your phone as soon as you get home in
the evening (then unplugging it before going to bed) is
a much better idea.

9 SEE THE LIGHT

If you have ever changed a light bulb, you'll know that, as well as light, a traditional bulb gives off an awful lot of heat.

The incandescent light bulb was invented more than a hundred years ago, and since then scientists have come up with much more efficient ways of producing light from electricity.

Fluorescent bulbs work by using electricity to make a white phosphor coating on the inside of the glass glow. They are so much more efficient than traditional bulbs – and last so much longer – that each one will save you more than fifteen times its cost in electricity bills and replacement bulbs over its lifetime. Each household has on average twenty-three light bulbs, so changing them all to energy-saving lamps could save you a huge amount of money (and a lot of time changing light bulbs over the years).

Compact fluorescent bulbs contain small amounts of mercury, so if one does stop working, make sure you take it to the recycling centre rather than put it in the bin.

A more recent invention is the light-emitting diode (LED). This is a simple electronic component that converts electricity directly into light. LEDs are very energy efficient and last ten times longer than even compact fluorescent bulbs.

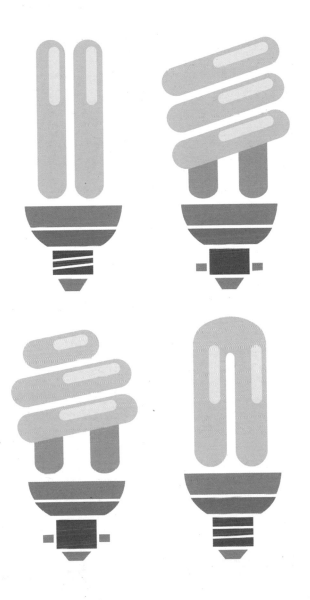

GREEN ELECTRICITY

Generating electricity without burning fossil fuels will be an essential part of our future, and there are a whole range of different ways of doing this – from the windmills that have been around for years, to newer technologies that harness solar, tidal and wave power. These are all called renewable technologies, because the fuel they use renews itself naturally. Neither fossil fuels nor uranium for nuclear power are renewable and will eventually run out.

Some countries are taking a lead on green energy. People in Germany were making and buying half the world's solar panels in 2005, because the government made sure electricity produced by solar power received a high price on the power market. Similar support for the wind industry in Denmark means that four in ten of the world's wind turbines are produced there.

Some green tariffs, available from electricity companies, can help provide investment for new renewable energy projects. And even if you don't get preferential rates that make it profitable in the short term, generating electricity at home is more and more viable as technology improves.

There are a range of different technologies – some new and others very old – which can be used to provide green electricty. Wind power has been used for centuries (think sailing boats and windmills) but only recently has it contributed to generating electricity. There is also huge potential in wave and tidal power. However, this is still at quite an early stage of development and is only just starting to attract investment. Energy from the sun is another renewable source of free energy. In particularly sunny areas of the world, solar energy can generate as much electricity as a power station. California, for example, aims to build a million solar roofs over the next ten years.

Geo-thermal power also has a role to play in the electricity mix. Take Iceland, which has many volcanoes and gets nearly a third of its electricity from geo-thermal power. Renewable electricity can also be generated using biofuels – Ely Power Station in Cambridgeshire in the UK burns waste agricultural straw, and is the largest of its kind in the world.

10 BUY GREENER ELECTRICITY

Not so long ago, if you signed up to a green electricity tariff that promised to buy 100 per cent renewable electricity to match the amount you used, carbon calculator websites would let you write off the carbon footprint of all your electricity.

But it turned out not to be quite that simple. Rather than give higher market rates to green electricity, the UK government opted for a different policy called the Renewables Obligation. This meant that all electricity companies had to buy a certain proportion of their electricity from renewable generators.

With this policy in place, it is possible for people buying green tariffs not to make any difference to the amount of renewable energy being produced. This is because some electricity companies simply allocate the green energy they have to buy under the Renewables Obligation to these customers' accounts.

Finding the right green tariff

It's important to check what your electricity company does to convert your money into new windmills and solar panels. Some companies invest some of your money directly into new projects, while others don't count some of your green electricity as part of the Renewables Obligation.

Ethical Consumer magazine gives each a simple rating to help you make up your mind (www.ethiscore.com). In 2007, the National Consumer Council also produced a report called 'Reality or Rhetoric', which rated the different tariffs available (www.ncc.org.uk).

GENERATE YOUR OWN ENERGY

Both large- and small-scale green energy projects will be essential in providing our electricity needs in the future. By generating renewable energy at home, you can reduce your bills, help support a new industry and cut your carbon emissions.

Different technologies are suitable for different homes, so do get expert advice before purchasing any kit. If you have a large, south-facing roof, solar panels might be the best thing for you, or if you live on an exposed hillside, a small wind turbine might be viable.

Grants to help install renewable energy at home are also available from the government, although they are usually in short supply

In the UK, the Energy Saving Trust and the Low Carbon Buildings Programme can help find expert advice and any available grants. Visit their websites for more information:

www.energysavingtrust.org.uk
www.lowcarbonbuildings.org.uk

SAVING ENERGY
IN THE KITCHEN

Combined, our cooking and our use of 'cold' and 'wet' appliances, such as fridges and washing machines, add up to almost half the electricity consumed in our homes.

The kitchen is therefore a great place to look for energy-saving ideas, and there's a lot more you can do than simply buy A-rated machines. Many of the best ideas are about changing how we use and maintain our appliances.

The more clever features that are built into electronic gadgets, the greater the danger they will use power even when they aren't helping us in the kitchen.

The base units for modern jug kettles may have a power indicator light, or even new settings such as 'keep warm', which mean they keep on using power after boiling the kettle. That fancy display to show the water level could also draw a constant stream of electricity when the kettle is not in use.

Almost all microwaves and toasters, as well as other gadgets such as grills and mixers, have clocks and electronic displays that use standby power. Some kitchens even have built-in televisions, so don't forget to turn those off as well.

12 COOL DOWN YOUR FRIDGE

Next to heating up the house, keeping perishables cold is one of the most energy-intensive activities in the home.

The best way of turning a fridge into an energy hog is to leave the door open. Because it takes heat from the inside and pushes it out into the room, if you were to open the fridge and then leave the room for a few hours, you would find it had actually heated up the whole kitchen (I'm not recommending this experiment!).

Try to get into the habit of thinking about what you want from the fridge before opening the door, rather than doing your meal planning while the fridge motor goes into overdrive.

Another useful and inexpensive gadget is a saver plug that replaces the normal plug on a fridge. This will limit the power consumption of the fridge's coolant pump.

In a simple fridge control system, the pump keeps working at full power until the effects have been felt throughout the fridge and turned it off at the thermostat. However, running the motor for this long isn't necessary and will actually cool the fridge below the target temperature in the end. Having a saver plug is like adding a more sophisticated control panel to your fridge that prevents unnecessary over-cooling.

These plugs aren't suitable for fridges that have electronic controls (these are more efficient already) or ice-makers (not so helpful), so check the list in the small print before you buy one.

13 FRIDGE AND FREEZER TIPS

Try these other simple tips to keep your cold food eco-friendly:

• Buy a fridge or freezer no bigger than you need.

• Keep them away from your boiler and oven, or they will have to work harder than necessary.

• Keep freezers as full as possible, but empty the fridge of old items regularly. These tips both reduce the energy needed to keep things at the right temperature.

• Never put warm items into a fridge or freezer. Wait for food to cool down to room temperature first.

• Defrost fridges and freezers regularly, as a build-up of ice makes them run less efficiently.

• Remove dust from the condenser coils at the back, so they can quickly radiate the heat away from the appliance.

• Check your door seals – a piece of paper should stay stuck in the seal even if tugged gently. If you have a fridge or freezer that regularly ices up, the seals may well be at fault – and costing you a fortune, too.

WASHING AND DRYING

14

The newer your washing machine, the more likely it is to be an efficient A-rated machine, or higher. In the UK now, more than 90 per cent of new washing machines sold are rated A or above.

However, these ratings – and any other eco-friendly claims made by the manufacturer – will be based on the most eco-friendly washing cycle, so it is really important that you use it.

Use the eco-cycle

The energy-saving washing cycle may take a bit longer to run, but waiting an extra twenty minutes for your washing is rarely a problem. Use the eco-cycle whenever you can and you'll make the most of your green machine.

Fill up properly

The test cycles are also based on using a full load. You've probably heard before that you should run a full load in the washing machine, but even I was surprised to find out that, in technical terms, a full load literally means filling the machine up. While your instinct may be to leave the clothes with room to breathe, it's far better to pile them in right to the top.

Don't dry unless you have to

Tumbledrying is often not necessary and most people manage to do without it. Only two in five households own a tumbledrier, and these are only used for around half of all washes.

15 COOKING

If you have ever used a camping stove, you'll know that, out on a windy hillside, you would never try to boil water in an uncovered pan. Letting all that heat escape could mean waiting for an hour just for a cup of tea, as well as using up most of your fuel.

At 15 per cent of all home electricity, there is a lot of scope for saving energy while we cook. Let's apply some campsite principles to our kitchens.

• Use the right size pan for your food, and the right size ring or burner for the pan.

• Use a lid on saucepans for faster cooking, which also uses less energy.

• Don't overfill the pan with water; just enough to cover the food is fine, especially if you use a lid to catch the evaporation.

- Use the kettle to boil water for cooking, rather than heating it up in the pan. The only time you shouldn't do this is if you are boiling cold eggs from the fridge, as these may crack from the shock of having boiling water poured over them.

- Only fill the kettle with as much water as you need right then.

- Pasta will cook without being held at a rolling boil. Add pasta to hot water, bring it back to the boil and then turn off the heat and put on a tight-fitting lid. After the normal cooking time, you should find the pasta is ready to eat.

16 BUY LOCAL

International trade in food almost trebled between the 1960s and 1990s, and a simple basket of fresh food can have travelled as much as 100,000 miles on its way to the supermarket.

All these extra miles are not due to our taste for exotic foods, but because of increasingly open trade rules. Larger multinational companies can cope with large transport costs while still charging low prices, because they can source foods from areas with cheap labour and lower farming costs, and because they can drive a hard bargain with suppliers.

Green campaigners have exposed the 'great food swap' that happens within Europe, where there are now very few trade barriers – the UK now exports almost as much chicken, lamb and pork to the Netherlands as it imports from the Netherlands.

Long-distance trade should be reserved for non-basics you can't grow at home (such as spices and tea, which have been traded internationally for centuries). And what we do import should be transported by ship where possible. Kilogram for kilogram, sea transport is about five times less carbon intensive than taking freight by road, and more than thirty times more efficient than flying it in.

EAT OR GROW ORGANIC 17

Because food is grown, caught or collected out in the environment, there can be other problems to contend with, not just the carbon cost of transport.

Organic farming aims to grow food without artificial pesticides and fertilisers, and work in balance with the land and wildlife. Policies to encourage organic farming are in place in many countries, and businesses are stocking more and more organic food. This is largely as a consequence of increased consumer demand, so keep it up!

Beware of organic food that has travelled long distances. Solving one environmental problem just to make another one worse isn't really what this is all about.

Labelling can be confusing, too. It has always seemed strange to me that shops save their green packaging for organic products, while their local produce doesn't get this accolade. If in doubt, trust your instincts and eat locally and seasonally where possible. That way, outside the tomato season you won't have to worry about whether to get hot-house tomatoes from close to home or organic ones from far away.

Of course, you can also have delicious, seasonal, organic food by growing your own. See the garden section of this book for some great tips on creating your own organic kitchen garden.

18 DON'T WASTE GOOD FOOD

My mum used make me finish my plate by saying, 'Don't you know there are children in the world who won't have any dinner tonight!' Thirty years later and tragically this is still the case, but these days she could add another admonishment, 'Don't you know how much carbon dioxide went into making that!'

Farming (even organic farming) uses fossil fuels to work the fields, and all our food needs oil to be transported to factories, to the shops, and then to our kitchens.

In response to people like us wanting more information about the things we buy, food producers are now trying to count the carbon cost of their products. A crisp manufacturer has completed its calculations and discovered that one 25g packet of its crisps is responsible for 75g of carbon dioxide in the atmosphere.

All of this makes it very important not just to buy food with a lower carbon footprint, but also not to waste the food we buy. In terms of its impact, reducing food waste could do more good than all the efforts you make to eat more eco-friendly foods.

We waste more than we think

A research project in England asked people to keep a diary of what they put in the bin. The people involved mostly had mums like mine and felt guilty about the amount of leftovers they threw away, but they were shocked to find out how much other food they wasted as well.

The total – including vegetable peelings, bones, spoiled food from the fridge, rotten fruit, stale bread and many other things – was more than a third of all the food they bought, and much more than the amount of packaging waste.

At least half this food could have been eaten if it had been managed better. And it's not just a waste of resources; the cost of all the food we throw away in a lifetime could add up to a year's salary.

Why are we throwing away so much food?

One of the major reasons is unplanned shopping trips. If we arrive at the supermarket without a list, and without checking our cupboards first, some of the ingredients will end up going bad before they are used.

And more than half of us who do make lists abandon them when we are tempted by special 'buy one get one free' offers.

Once we get it all home, we are also not very good at storing perishable foods, or at eating the oldest things first.

We can learn a lot from older generations on this score, perhaps because they can remember when food wasn't piled up high at low, low prices.

Older people are far more likely to cook meals from scratch and to shop in an organised fashion. The most wasteful groups are young, working single people (living on your own with irregular hours can ruin meal planning) and families with young children (not surprisingly, shopping with a child makes sticking to a list even harder).

Tips to reduce food waste
Don't worry, you don't need to become housekeeper of the year to cut down on food waste. Just thinking about the problem can help develop better habits. Try some of these tips to make a bigger difference.

• Make shopping lists (and look in the cupboard before setting off for the shops) to avoid buying things you already have in stock. Online shopping can help with this, as these services will often let you keep lists of what you recently bought on file.

• Buy more loose fruit and vegetables, so you can buy just the right amount for the recipes you are making. Salad vegetables are the most commonly wasted, so buy these on the day from your local shops, rather than on your weekly trip to the supermarket.

• Keep your fridge at the right temperature – between one and five degrees will keep food fresher for longer.

• Look at the use-by dates, and eat things in date order.

And don't forget, almost all the unavoidable waste can be used to feed your garden if you put it in the compost. More about this in the gardening section of this book.

CUT DOWN ON MEAT 9

'Hang on,' I hear you say, 'this isn't supposed to be about being more ethical. It's about being greener. Leave my bacon sandwiches out of it!'. Well, this section isn't as out of place as you might think. The fact is, eating less meat is very, very good for the planet.

I'm not actually a proper vegetarian, but I am a very light consumer of meat. Sometimes I will go for a whole week without any animal parts reaching my plate, and if I do eat meat, it's only likely to be a bit of fish or the odd slice of salami. The reason I do this is almost completely environmental.

A lot of the problem is the burps and farts. Farmed cows and sheep are responsible for nearly two fifths of the total quantity of methane generated by human activity. As a greenhouse gas, methane trumps carbon dioxide many times over (though it doesn't stay in the atmosphere as long), so the contribution of animal farming to climate change is substantial.

Rearing animals, calorie for calorie, also uses far more land and water than growing vegetarian food. Thousands of litres of water and seven kilograms of cereal feed are used in the process of making just one kilogram of beef.

Think about it: we're growing crops to feed animals to feed us. It's a madly inefficient way of using the world's resources.

Think vegetarian

A lot of vegetarian food is also much healthier for you. So if you're watching your fat intake or cholesterol, eating more vegetable dishes can help a lot.

There have been strict vegetarians throughout history – from Plato to Paul McCartney – and some whole religions urge their followers to abstain from meat. If you go completely veggie, you will be in good company.

But the best thing about eating vegetarian food for environmental reasons is that it doesn't have to be an 'all or nothing' thing.

Every meal you eat without meat will help to reduce climate change, and to preserve water and land for better uses. Bearing this in mind when looking at a menu is a far less daunting prospect than taking a pledge never to eat another steak ever again.

Try new ingredients

I have recently discovered that those two veggie staples – lentils and tofu – have a completely undeserved reputation. They are actually delicious when cooked in good recipes.

Tofu is great in a stir-fry if you marinate it first in soy sauce and as much garlic and ginger as you can handle. Then stir-fry the tofu in hot oil until it browns before adding the rest of the vegetables and sauce ingredients.

Lentil soup is nice, but my favourite recipe is a salad made with green lentils and vegetables all drenched in a vinaigrette dressing.

Be more adventurous in your menu choices and find loads of recipe suggestions online.

• The Vegetarian Society has a wealth of suggestions, plus advice on a balanced diet: www.vegsoc.org

• The BBC food's website keeps a massive stock of recipes, many from famous chefs: www.bbc.co.uk/food

• Chinese, Indian and Middle Eastern cuisines have always made excellent use of vegetarian ingredients, such as lentils, beans and tofu, as well as lots of interesting vegetable dishes. If you pick only meat dishes from your local takeaway menu, you're missing out on some gorgeous – and classic – alternatives.

SAVING WATER IN THE HOME

Climate change will have a profound effect on fresh water around the world. Many areas, such as the western coast of South America and the Indian subcontinent, depend on water from huge glaciers to fill their rivers. As snowfall reduces and these glaciers recede, this will cause water shortages for billions of people.

Western Europe and the Atlantic coast of the USA are likely to see dry weather accompanied by dramatic storms, with rainfall coming in very concentrated bursts. This will make flash floods more likely at the same time as water shortages.

Where I live in London, we already have less rainfall than Istanbul, and more and more people are moving into the city, making the conservation of water a top priority. But with clean, fresh water on tap twenty-four hours a day, we tend to take this precious resource for granted.

Cleaning water to a drinkable standard takes lots of energy and several chemicals, yet only about 4 per cent of the fresh water in the average home is used for drinking and cooking. Most is used for purposes where drinking quality isn't required.

In the future, we will make far more use of 'grey water' (rainwater and water that has previously been used for washing) for things such as flushing the toilet. New eco-homes are having grey-water systems fitted as standard, but there are lots of other ways to cut down on the amount of water we waste at home.

You can also reuse grey water to save water outside the home. See the garden section of this book for more about saving water in the garden.

20 WASHING DISHES

I've lost count of the number of arguments I have had about whether washing up by hand or using a dishwasher is better for the planet. But now, after several attempts to work it out on the back of an envelope in the pub, I have finally found a sensible answer on the excellent Waterwise website (www.waterwise.org.uk).

It turns out that it all depends on your style of washing up. If, like a friend of mine, you believe that half the cleaning is done by the tea towel at the end, you probably use less water and energy washing up by hand than you would with a machine. However, if you pre-rinse, wash, then fastidiously rinse every plate, cup and dish under a running tap, you might want to find an efficient dishwasher to do the job instead.

Whichever method you use, you can save both water and energy by following these simple tips:

By hand:
• Use a bowl, not running water.
• Don't rinse everything for ages; use eco-friendly washing-up liquid and you won't need to worry so much about toxic residues.

By machine:
• Pick a water- and energy-efficient model – both ratings are summarised on the label in the showroom.
• Wipe waste food off dishes before putting them in the machine. Don't rinse under the tap.
• Always run the machine with a full load.

SHOWER POWER 21

We all know that taking a shower rather than a bath saves water. The vast majority of people now have a shower in their home – up from just a fifth in the 1970s.

However, a long time spent in a modern power shower can easily go through more water than a bath, and about 12 per cent of our water use now takes place while we are showering.

You can save more than half this water simply by switching your shower head. An aerating shower head mixes air into the flow to keep the pressure high but reduce the water used. Low-flow showerheads use less water, but at a higher pressure, so you can save water without even noticing.

In the summer, when the garden needs water, take a bucket into the shower and place it near your feet. It will soon fill up with grey water that you can pour over your thirsty plants outside, without using up extra supplies.

22 TOILET TRAINING

Flushing the toilet is responsible for about 30 per cent of all the water we go through in the home.

Toilets vary hugely in the amount of water they use per flush – pre-1950s models can use up to thirteen litres, whereas modern cisterns only hold about six litres. Newer toilets also have a dual-flush option, with a smaller button that can be used when there is less to flush away.

And then there's the 'deep green' option of not flushing every time. It's actually not essential to flush unless you've made a deposit of solid matter. However, adopting this habit is unlikely to make you popular unless you live on your own or with very close friends!

If you have a large, old toilet, you can save a litre of water every time you flush, without affecting performance, by adding a simple water-saving device, for example a 'hippo', to the cistern. This is basically just a container that retains some of the water in the cistern rather than pouring it away.

Leaks can also increase a toilet's impact on water consumption. Check for a leaky loo by adding food colouring to the cistern. If you can see the colour in the bowl after an hour or two, you've got a leak, so call in a plumber to fix it.

REUSE AND RECYCLE

This topic is usually the first thing that springs to mind when we think about being green.

Most of us are well aware of the need to recycle, and we are getting quite good at it (although we are often constrained by the facilities available nearby). People in the Netherlands, Austria, Germany and Belgium are now recycling more than half their waste, and even in the UK, where we only recycle 18 per cent of our rubbish, three quarters of us do at least some recycling.

But there's much more we can do. More than 90 per cent of all the material in our bins could be used again, and we need to reclaim all of this if we are going to be able to call ourselves 'zero waste'.

Sending waste to the recycling plant rather than the landfill site doesn't just save materials; it also saves a huge amount of energy. The amount you can save as a diligent recycler might come as a bit of a shock: recycling just one aluminium can saves enough energy to run your TV for three hours.

That's because extracting new aluminium is a very energy intensive process. Similarly, making new glass takes a lot more energy than melting down an old bottle – and, of course, it's even better to refill and reuse a bottle, too.

In total, the materials the average family throws away in a year could be recycled to save enough energy to take 3,500 showers.

And recycling isn't the only answer. Cutting down on the amount of waste we create in the first place is even more important.

23 DON'T BRING IT HOME

It's easy to reduce the amount of waste material you bring home in the first place. After all, why carry something home if you are going to chuck it straight in the bin?

Some European countries let you leave excess packaging in the shop for the company to recycle. If you're feeling militant, you could try this at your local supermarket! If not, then just try these simple ideas:

• Take reusable cloth bags or durable plastic bags to the shops, or just some pre-used carrier bags. Lots of designers are now creating shopping bags that are both comfortable to carry and fashionable.

• Choose goods with less packaging, particularly loose food such as fresh fruit and vegetables.

• Use local bakeries that put cakes and pastries in paper or cardboard instead of layers of plastic (shopping locally helps the planet in other ways, too).

• At the checkout, don't put more plastic around packaged goods such as meat and cheese.

• If you're having a party, use glasses and real cutlery, not plastic cups, knives and forks. Many shops will lend you extra glasses when you buy your drinks.

REFILL
AND REUSE 24

There was once a real culture of reusable packaging. When I was a little girl, milk, fizzy drinks and eggs were all sold door-to-door in refillable containers, but nowadays there are far fewer of these businesses around.

However, many cleaning products and cosmetics are now being produced in refillable containers, and luckily these are often the less polluting products as well.

You can also help by reusing items for a different purpose. Plastic takeaway boxes make great containers for packed lunches, and many items can find a new life in the garden as well. (See the garden section of this book for more tips.)

25 CLOSE THE LOOP

Of course, sending things for recycling is fine, but where do they go after that? Materials can only be reused if there is a demand for them, and most of the demand for plastic is currently in the Far East – a long way from your local recycling centre.

However, more products than you might think are already being made from recycled materials closer to home.

- Newspapers are made from 80 per cent recycled paper.
- Almost all cardboard boxes are made from recycled material.
- Green bottles made in the UK are 85 per cent recycled glass.

New products made from recycled plastic are being launched all the time. Look out for bin liners, plastic bottles, pencils, flooring, fencing, water butts, window frames, files and folders, garden furniture and even clothing.

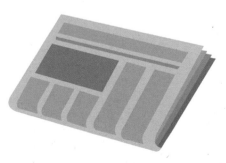

LEARN YOUR LOGOS 26

It's useful to know that most plastic is embossed with its recycling number.

 PET – polyethylene terephthalate. Used for drinks bottles and food packaging.

 HDPE – high-density polyethylene. Bottles of milk and cleaning products.

 PVC – polyvinyl chloride. Bottles for drinks and shampoo, clingfilm and food packaging.

 LDPE – low-density polyethylene. Bags and bin liners.

 PP – polypropylene. Margarine containers, stationery items, food boxes and trays.

 PS – polystyrene. Foam packaging, vending cups, egg cartons, plastic knives and forks.

 Others – any other plastics not in these categories.

Plastics 1 to 5 are all easily recyclable, but plastic 6 is often not taken by local recycling services. Some local guides aren't very clear: when they say 'only plastic bottles', this might mean they can only recycle plastics 1, 2 and 3. So they may be able to take other items if they are made of these plastics. It's worth asking them to clarify their guides to help everyone recycle more.

27 NO-HEAP COMPOSTING

Even if you don't have a garden or the space for a big compost bin, you can still deal with your kitchen waste by employing some worms – nature's own high-speed composting units.

Worm composting is far quicker than using an ordinary bin in the garden. It is also far less smelly – so much so that several people I know keep their wormeries indoors. Wormeries produce a rich compost and a liquid plant food that are both ideal for use in pots and window boxes.

Don't worry, you don't have to handle the worms; just drop your vegetable peelings, egg shells, kitchen towels and tea bags into the wormery and forget about it.

Wormeries are increasingly popular all over the world. Almost one in twenty Australian households already has one, and worm composting is catching on in American cities, too.

For indoor use, a well-sealed commercial wormery kit is best, unless you want to risk a worm escape in your kitchen. Outdoors, it's easier to improvise and build your own. The worms don't really need any special treatment – after all, it's what they do naturally.

DEMAND LESS WASTE 28

Reducing waste is an area where individuals can do a lot, but our efforts are constrained by the actions companies and governments take to back them up.

Give your support to campaigns calling for a plastic bag tax (this has worked a treat in Ireland where the use of plastic bags has gone down more than 90%) and for regulations such as Germany's 'green dot' scheme. This makes producers buy rights for packaging according to weight, creating a real incentive for them to cut down.

If a favourite product has too much packaging, exercise your consumer elbow by writing to the company and pointing this out. Companies are likely to listen more carefully to a loyal customer than to a protestor with a placard.

BE A GREENER CLEANER

These days, our homes contain a multitude of specialist cleaning products: two bottles for the dishwasher, another two for our clothes, one product to clean the kitchen surfaces, one for the bath, one for the floor... the list goes on and on.

Do we really need all these different chemicals? Isn't there a simpler, greener way to keep our homes grime-free?

The first cleaning product was soap. Made by reacting oils with alkali salts to create molecules that are attracted to both water and grease, soap helps suspend dirt in water to make it easier to wash away.

Soap was invented more than 3,000 years ago, but only became popular in the nineteenth century, when adverts promoting health and cleanliness created famous brands.

Soap has been gradually replaced in the home by synthetic detergents based on petrol. They have evolved quickly and 'improved' versions now hit our supermarket shelves every week – many far more powerful than necessary for household cleaning

The main environmental problem with these products is that they do not degrade efficiently when poured down the drain, causing pollution. At the treatment plant, up to 20,000 litres of water is used to deal with one kilogram of washing powder, and the end products still end up in our waterways, where they can accumulate in wildlife.

Luckily, there are simple solutions for keeping our homes clean without filling our cupboards – and the environment – with doubtful chemicals.

29 GREENER CLEANERS

Keep your cupboards simple by cutting down on specialist products. For most cleaning jobs, one bottle of multipurpose detergent will do the trick.

Buy ecological cleaning products
Look out for biodegradable dishwashing liquids and washing powders based on easily broken down, plant-based ingredients.

• Avoid artificial fragrances in cleaning products. Green products contain only natural fragrances, or none at all.

• Buy products that can be refilled wherever possible.

Avoid harsh chemicals for unblocking sinks. Use a plunger instead

1. First loosen grease by pouring boiling water down the blocked sink.

2. If this doesn't solve the problem, get a plunger and fill the sink with a few inches of water.

3. Cover the overflow outlet with one hand to maintain the pressure, then plunge firmly to force water down the pipe.

Problem solved, and no chemicals involved!

ASK GRANNY 30

Many old-fashioned home tips from our grandparents are time-saving and cheap, and use things commonly found around the home. Your relatives will enjoy being asked for their own ideas, but here's a few to start with:

• Clean windows using warm water with a squirt of washing up liquid and a dash of vinegar, then polish dry with newspaper for a streak-free shine.

• Light a match in the loo to burn off bad smells – it really works. Elsewhere, open windows or burn candles, rather than use chemical sprays to mask odours.

Removing stains largely depends on treating them quickly – most liquids won't stain if you soak them up quickly and then wash with normal soap. Or try these tips straight from *Mrs Beeton's Book of Household Management* (1923 edition):

• Wash out mud stains in water that has been used to boil potatoes.

• Scrub a stained chopping board with sea salt and lemon juice (also great for softening hands).

• Dip red wine stains on linen into hot milk for a few minutes before washing.

• Clean brown leather boots and bags with the inside of a banana skin, then polish with a soft cloth (makes them smell interesting, too!).

GREENER DIY

We're all familiar with 'new car smell' which is due to gases given off by all the plastics and upholstery in a newly made vehicle. You have probably also heard of 'sick building syndrome' in connection with offices. Long hours spent in rooms with poor ventilation, surrounded by synthetic materials that leach chemicals into the air, can cause a range of health problems for sensitive workers.

Refurbishing your house with new carpets, new paint on the walls, and new furniture and fittings can bring a host of problematic chemicals and eco-destructive materials into your living space as well.

The solution isn't to move out and live in a tepee. There are many substitutes for synthetic, chemical-based materials (often the materials the synthetic versions substituted in the first place!) to help you with a stylish home redesign that won't harm you or the planet.

3 | CLEANER PAINTS

Conventional emulsion and gloss paint is a cocktail of toxic chemicals. The solvents used in paints are known as volatile organic compounds (or VOCs), but there's nothing nice or organic about them. They are chemicals derived from oil, which can cause eye irritation or respiratory problems in vulnerable people – and they aren't particularly good for everyone else either.

Even after conventional paint is dry, it can still give off chemicals, such as formaldehyde and benzene, none of which makes for a healthy home environment.

Low-VOC alternative paints are available by mail order and are even stocked by some big DIY chains. Look on the label for emulsion paints with less than 50g/litre of VOCs, or 150g/litre for gloss. Even better are zero-VOC paints with less than 5g/litre.

Eco-paints can be slightly more expensive, but come with additional benefits. They are not smelly to use, go on beautifully and brushes can be cleaned with water afterwards.

SUSTAINABLE WOOD 32

One of the earliest environmental problems I can remember being aware of is the loss of forests around the world, particularly tropical rainforests. More and more is being done to legally protect ancient forests, but deforestation – much of it illegal – is still going on at an enormous rate.

Unfortunately, illegally logged timber products are widely available in the shops. The easiest way to be certain you aren't supporting illegal logging is to make sure everything you buy is certified by the Forest Stewardship Council.

But don't be put off using timber altogether. A good wooden floor can last a lifetime, saving many replacement carpets, and timber is usually the best choice for new windows. Not only is wood less toxic to make and live with than PVC, it is also more durable. And it is much easier to repair a wooden window frame than to deal with a PVC unit that may need replacing altogether when one part fails.

Inside the home, treat wooden fittings and furniture with beeswax or plant oils, rather than varnish. These products smell great and give a much nicer, warmer finish – with no dodgy petrochemicals.

33 GREENER FLOORS

The most popular floor coverings are carpet and PVC lino, but these are among the least healthy and green things you can put on your floors. Carpets contain surprisingly high levels of toxic chemicals, including flame-retardants and pesticides, as well as VOCs from adhesives, backings and synthetic yarns.

Chemicals known as phthalates are used to soften PVC vinyl flooring and these are the most common environmental pollutant. When burned, PVC also releases dioxins, which can cause cancer, disrupt hormones and stay in ecosystems for years.

Luckily, the alternatives to carpet and PVC aren't just less toxic, they are also more attractive, more stylish and nicer to live with, and are often great solutions for allergy sufferers, too.

Make sure whatever floor covering you choose is tacked down, not glued and this will help with recycling it later.

Real lino and natural rubber

Real 'linoleum' is made from renewable materials: wood powder, linseed oil, pine resin, cork and chalk, usually with a jute backing.

Flooring made from natural rubber is another alternative to PVC. Rubber tapping does not kill trees and the final product can also be recycled.

Both rubber and lino are good for allergy sufferers, and are far less toxic, more durable and more sustainable than vinyl.

Bamboo

Bamboo is one of the most versatile and eco-friendly materials for the home, as people in the East have long known. It is strong, attractive and durable, and has a huge range of uses, from strong furniture structure to soft fibres suitable for clothing.

It is one of the fastest-growing plants in the world, with some of the biggest varieties of this super grass putting on a metre of growth in a day. There are types of bamboo that will grow almost everywhere in the world, so you can find local supplies, and it is often grown without pesticides or fertilisers.

An increasing number of companies are making and selling bamboo products for the home, because of its unique combination of usefulness and green credentials. Look out for bamboo flooring, worktops, window blinds, kitchenware, bathroom items and furniture (particularly garden furniture).

Other natural floor coverings

There are a whole host of natural plant fibres that are being used to create interesting, beautiful and tactile floor coverings. Look out for materials made from jute (also known as hessian), sisal (from the leaves of a large succulent plant), coir (from the husks of coconuts), a wide range of grasses, and hemp – one of the most versatile eco-materials around.

34 RECLAIM AND REFURBISH

Reclaiming items for your home can be hugely satisfying, and can also make your home unique. I love the style of the 1950s but, whichever period you prefer, old pieces of furniture, lamps and other accessories can be far nicer than new, lightweight pieces.

I buy second-hand furniture wherever possible, and after a quick sanding or a lick of paint, it is as good as new and has far more character than a plain, anonymous product from a superstore.

Antique shops and auctions sometimes have designer bargains from the twentieth century. Flea markets, car boot sales and even front gardens can be excellent sources of unwanted, high-quality heirlooms. People also put the most extraordinary things into skips. I have an excellent side table made from the tubular legs of a stool I got from a local skip.

If you're not very hands-on, don't worry. Sanding down and oiling an old coffee table really doesn't involve more effort than following all those instructions that come with a flat-pack item.

Hire tools, don't buy them
Buying tools you don't really need is a waste of all the resources and energy that went into making them, but the real problem is that consumer versions of power tools are usually under-powered and not really very good.

BEING GREENER IN THE GARDEN

A garden can help reduce your carbon footprint in lots of ways.

Having a beautiful outside space to lounge in rather than driving off to the country is fantastic, and growing some of your own food can make a real difference to the carbon footprint of your daily diet as well.

Another big difference your garden can make is helping the local environment by providing food and shelter for insects, birds and other creatures. You don't need acres of space to have an impact on wildlife, and even if you have no garden at all, you can still raise a range of crops in window boxes. A small balcony can be an effective kitchen garden, where you can grow some real luxuries for your plate.

Gardening does have its environmental pitfalls, so a green-fingered 'green' will be careful about water use in the garden, and won't use lots of chemicals.

Luckily for lazy gardeners like me, following organic principles isn't difficult and an eco-friendly garden – working with nature, not against it – can actually be much less work to look after.

And unless you want your garden to turn into a gas-guzzler, don't even think about getting a patio heater!

GROWING FOOD AND FLOWERS

What better way to save carbon emissions and food miles, and ensure you have fresh food and flowers you can trust, than to grow your own?

Running a small kitchen garden needn't be a lot of hassle. The bit of tending and digging that it needs can be very therapeutic – and good for fitness, too. Even with a small patio garden or yard, you can still raise useful crops and flowers in containers and grow-bags.

The concept of food miles is gaining a lot of publicity, but flower miles is a less-talked-about environmental issue. More and more cut flowers are being flown in from hot countries, and out-of-season flowers from closer to home can also have a large carbon footprint if they are grown in heated greenhouses.

A simple solution is to raise flowering plants yourself, either in the garden or in a conservatory or greenhouse.

35 WHAT TO GROW

Which vegetables and flowers you grow in your garden is completely up to you. My philosophy is to grow fruit and vegetables that are either expensive luxuries in the shops, or which taste best when at their freshest. In my opinion, things such as peas and raspberries are the best-value crops to grow, as shop varieties are always a huge disappointment.

Also important is to work with the soil you have. Blueberries might sound like a great idea, but they need a particular kind of acidic soil, which will make caring for them a real hassle if you are in the wrong area.

Sourcing plants and seeds

You can buy an enormous variety of fruit and vegetable plants and seeds in garden centres, and there are more organically raised varieties on offer nowadays, too.

An excellent and cheap way to get new plants is to take cuttings from family, friends and neighbours. Plants that are successful locally may be more hardy to the conditions in your garden, and more resistant to the local population of pests as well.

MY LIST OF FAVOURITE THINGS TO GROW:

Fruit and vegetables
- Raspberries
- Peas
- Runner beans
- Strawberries
- Potatoes
- Tomatoes and courgettes
  (great in grow-bags, but need a lot of water)
- Lettuce and rocket
  (cut-and-come-again varieties are easy to look after)
- Herbs
  (bay, rosemary and mint need almost no tending at all
  and chives also have attractive flowers)

Flowers
- Tulips (including summer-flowering varieties)
- Daffodils
- Cornflowers
- Climbing roses
- Small sunflowers
- Bluebells
- Lavender (copes well with dry conditions)
- Lilies (some varieties will grow new flowers again and
  again after cutting)

36 CROP ROTATION

Growing the same vegetables in the same place every year can remove essential nutrients from the soil. Rotating crops each season helps to reduce this, and helps you to avoid artificial fertilisers, too.

Vegetables can be classified into four groups. Plant each section of your vegetable plot with plants from a different group and then rotate the groups each year. This way the soil can recover from the effects of one crop over the next three years when you are growing other things.

Group 1
Root vegetables, such as potatoes, parsnips, carrots, beetroot

Group 2
Cabbages, sprouts, broccoli and other brassicas

Group 3
Peas and beans

Group 4
Everything else, including salad veg

For a more formal kitchen garden, and especially if your soil is poor, raised beds can be an excellent choice, and make for a simple way to manage crop rotation. Build up brick borders or lay down recycled railway sleepers and fill the bed with rich soil and compost before planting up.

ALLOTMENTS

If you enjoy growing a few vegetables, and find you want more space, you might want to expand your efforts and get an allotment. This is becoming incredibly popular among people who want to reduce their carbon footprint and take up a fascinating new hobby.

There can be long waiting lists, and penalties for not cultivating all the space once you get it. A good idea, which can also be lots of fun, is sharing the labour (and the produce) with a group of local friends.

GROWING THINGS WITHOUT A GARDEN

Even if you have no outside space apart from a small balcony or roof terrace, or even if all you have are a few window ledges, you can still grow a range of useful crops.

37 RAISE YOUR OWN CROPS

SALADS

Window-box and balcony conditions are great for easy-to-grow salad vegetables, such as rocket and lettuce. These crops like a mixture of sun and shade. Away from the ground, the dreaded slugs and snails will find them difficult to track down as well.

Again, this is a great way to steer clear of some of the most wasteful supermarket vegetables. Bags of ready-prepared salads are expensive, don't last very long and are often washed in heavily chlorinated water before packing. Growing your own means you can have the very freshest, chemical-free salad leaves whenever you want them.

To grow salad veg, simply fill a window box with compost (make sure this is peat-free if you aren't making your own), use a pencil to create two shallow furrows and sow your seeds along it. Cover the seeds, water gently and leave for a few days. Once the seedlings are up, thin the rows to a few plants each and keep the soil just moist while the plants grow.

When you have finished your first crop, plant some more or choose cut-and-come-again varieties that will grow new leaves as you pick them.

FRUIT AND VEG

Tomatoes, potatoes and other vegetables will do well on a balcony or in a window box, but need a reasonable depth of soil and some attention to watering. Planting in grow-bags can help reduce water needs, and they are very easy to organise. After the tomatoes have finished, you can reuse the bags for another crop, such as lettuce.

Strawberries love being grown in pots and are a fantastic treat in the summer. You can even grow them in hanging baskets. With plenty of love and care, bushy varieties of tomatoes will also grow in a hanging basket - and look great as well.

Compact varieties of sweet peppers, chillies and courgettes will also enjoy conditions on a sunny balcony. To reduce the impact of wind if you are high up, netting around an exposed balcony will help.

HERBS

Herbs are ideal for window boxes and small gardens.

Shop-bought fresh herbs can have a huge carbon footprint, as they are often imported from faraway countries. Unless you get organically grown herbs, they may also have been grown using a lot of chemicals in order to get a quick crop.

You can avoid all this environmental damage by growing your own herbs, no matter how little space you have. Indeed, herbs such as mint are best suited to pots, as they have invasive roots that can spread and take over a border.

Several kinds of herbs can be grown together in one big pot, or with enough care, you can raise a wide variety of different plants in separate, smaller pots.

All the cooks' favourites are suitable for small pot gardens, including annuals such as basil and coriander and perennials such as mint, oregano, chives and sage.

On a sunny windowsill, summer plants such as basil, will grow through the winter, when supermarket herbs are being flown in from afar.

Other plants that do well indoors include sprouting seeds, such as mung beans and fenugreek, as well as that childhood staple, cress.

Don't forget flowers
A small terrace, window box or balcony kitchen garden doesn't have to be totally functional. Apply the 'companion planting' principles from the organic gardening chapter to deter pests as well as add more beauty to your display.

Combine lavender with thyme and rosemary in a sunny spot for a fragrant display that also supplies useful culinary herbs. All these plants are relatively tolerant to drought, reducing watering needs.

WATERING

Plants in pots do need more watering than if they are planted out in the garden. Using a mulch on your pots, such as bark, moist compost or gravel, reduces moisture loss due to evaporation, or add water-retaining crystals to the compost to help plants survive between waterings.

USE WASTE TO
FEED YOUR GARDEN

So many of the things we throw in the bin could have a new life in the garden.

Most types of food waste, as well as materials such as cardboard, can be composted down to improve your soil. And if you grow your own vegetables, you can keep the cycle going by feeding the peelings back to your compost heap afterwards.

Many other household items can be employed in the garden when they have reached the end of their useful life indoors.

One of my friends uses an old bookcase as a strawberry frame and has laid down broken plates and cups to create a path around her vegetable patch. Along with a wide range of improvised planters (including a big shopping bag planted up with courgettes), it gives her garden a unique style and charm all of its own.

38 COMPOST

Composting is the new recycling in the world of green living. More people are catching the composting bug every day, and the amount of waste composted in the UK went up 35 per cent between 2004 and 2005.

That's because composting is one of the easiest and most rewarding eco-friendly activities; doing an awful lot of good to save waste and giving a useful end product, with very little time or effort. Apart from all the personal benefits of a less smelly kitchen bin and better soil, the benefits of composting for the wider environment are enormous.

You might think the same processes that happen in your compost bin also occur in a rubbish dump. But landfill sites don't provide the right conditions for healthy, oxygenated rotting of organic waste. Instead, landfill encourages unhealthy 'anaerobic' decomposition, producing methane – a potent greenhouse gas.

The things we throw away can also make a rubbish dump so toxic than nothing rots at all. Scientists took samples from a massive landfill site serving New York City in 1988 and found six-year-old lettuces that were still green, as well as a hot dog – with bun – that had remained intact for sixteen years!

In contrast, a well-tended, well-fed compost bin is teeming with life, as healthy bugs and bacteria work to break down almost any organic material into a nutritious treat for your garden.

Getting started – containers

Although you can simply pile things up in a heap, it's easier and less tempting for pests to keep your compost in a container. You can usually get a simple compost bin with a lid for nothing from your local council, or pick one up at a garden centre.

If you opt for a traditional heap, keep it covered with an old piece of carpet, so that the compost doesn't dry out in hot weather.

Ingredients for a balanced diet

The best compost comes from feeding your bin a balanced diet containing a mixture of tough, slow-rotting material, softer materials such as food scraps, and 'activators'. On their own, activator ingredients would rot quickly to a slimy mess, but in a balanced mix, they help everything else to compost more quickly.

Examples of things to add to your compost bin:

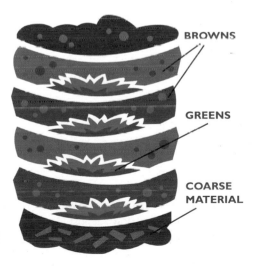

BROWNS

GREENS

COARSE MATERIAL

Activators to get it going
• Grass cuttings
• Weeds (avoid invasive weeds such as ground elder)
• Manure (from herbivorous animals)

Soft food for a nutritious mix
• Fruit and vegetable peelings
• Tea bags
• Coffee grounds
• Vacuum cleaner dust
• Hamster and gerbil bedding
• Dead flowers

Tough ingredients for body
- Hedge clippings
- Egg shells
- Straw
- Cardboard
- Dead leaves

Ingredients to avoid

Some ingredients can encourage unhealthy bacteria or pests, or can be toxic to the rest of the mix, so are best avoided. These include:
- Meat or fish, and cooked food
- Newspaper in large quantities, or glossy magazines
- Cat and dog waste, or nappies

Filling and tending your compost bin

Always start with a layer of twigs and cardboard to make sure the bottom of the heap is aerated. The whole compost bin needs air and bugs in order to rot effectively, so layering soft ingredients with tougher fibrous materials throughout the pile will help create channels to allow these helpful things into the centre.

A good idea is to keep some autumn leaves and hedge clippings next to your bin, and add a layer of these each time you top up with softer materials and activators. Imagine you're building a big green lasagne and you will be on the right lines.

The composting process will take several months, although you may find usable materials at the bottom of the bin quite quickly. The more you tend your compost, the quicker you will get results.

- To speed things up, turn the compost with a garden fork every few weeks to bring in air and encourage the good bugs to keep working.
- If you have added a lot of dry ingredients, you will need to water the compost occasionally to keep it moist.
- Don't put lots of grass cuttings in without mixing with other ingredients. Alternatively, use some of the grass to help activate leafmould (see page 94).
- A well-turned compost bin may heat up. This is the sign of really healthy compost. The heat even helps to kill any plant diseases that have gone in with the clippings.
- Chop up tough, woody stems before adding to the compost, unless you are using them to improve the structure.
- Urine is full of useful activator chemicals, and small amounts can speed up your composting. If you are a man, providing urine to your bin is fairly simple; ladies may need to use more ingenious methods.

When it's ready

Deciding when compost is ready isn't an exact science It may take two months or more than a year for your compost to rot down.

As a general rule of thumb, compost is ready to use whenever it looks useful. One day, when turning the compost, you will see dark brown material near the bottom. Dig this dark, earthy stuff out and use it, then mix up the rest and leave it to carry on composting. Chuck any recognisable lumps back in – it will all disappear eventually.

Use your compost all around the garden as a soil improver or to fill pots or trays for seedlings.

What about rats?

If there are rats in your area, they may come to investigate your compost bin, but making compost shouldn't lead to more rats than would otherwise be around. Help to discourage them by avoiding putting meat products in your bin and by using a bin with a lid, or surrounding a heap with chicken wire.

Make leafmould

Leafmould is a simple kind of compost made mainly from rotted, or partly rotted, autumn leaves. It is incredibly useful around the garden: use it to improve your soil, to mix with compost for potting plants, or as a mulch to help conserve water.

It's also very easy to make, needing virtually no tending at all. Almost any kind of autumn leaf will work, although some leaves, such as those from the plane tree (ubiquitous in my part of London), take more time than others.

The result is called leafmould, because autumn leaves are decomposed mainly by fungi rather than the bacteria that do most of the work in a compost bin. This process takes longer than composting, and a leafmould container is unlikely to heat up. Full rotting can take more than two years, although you can speed up the process by shredding the leaves first.

How to make leafmould:

1. Collect autumn leaves (not from evergreens, and not from under hedges, where they provide shelter for wildlife).
2. Mix in a few grass clippings.
3. Put in a container (a box, bin or a plastic sack with holes in).
4. Leave alone for up to two years.

Young leafmould (1–2 years old) can be used as mulch. Properly rotted leafmould can be used anywhere in the garden or mixed with compost (or even used on its own) for growing seeds.

REUSE IN THE GARDEN 39

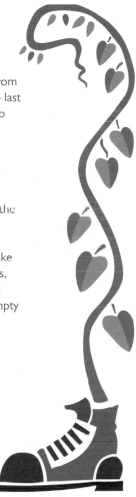

You should never need to buy a newly manufactured plant container for your garden. The materials they are made from – wood, cement, ceramics and metal – last for centuries (or millennia, as visitors to the British Museum can testify).

Second-hand shops and architectural salvage merchants have huge stocks of reclaimed items suitable for planting, edging, paving and many other uses in the garden.

Your garden is also a great place to make use of non-recyclable household goods, such as yogurt pots (made from plastic no. 6 – see page 59), leaky buckets, empty paint tins, old sinks or even furniture.

SUPPORTING WILDLIFE IN THE GARDEN

Most people today want a low-maintenance garden, which has led to a profusion of paved gardens, covered in decking or gravel.

The sparseness of today's gardens, with 'untidy' trees and hedges removed, non-native planting, and the use of powerful weedkillers and pesticides, has contributed to a dramatic reduction in the amount and range of wildlife in many of our towns and cities.

The loss of the house sparrow in London is a classic example of the harm done. Fifty years ago you could see them everywhere, but now the reduction in suitable nesting sites and feeding opportunities has put them on the RSPB's red list – the sparrow is now classified as a species in rapid decline.

Your garden can help bring sparrows and other wildlife back into our towns and cities by providing a haven for hard-pressed plants, insects and animals.

This is an area of green activity where your efforts on their own can make a real, visible difference. Local fauna and flora will seek out your efforts and you will be amazed at the variety of wildlife you can attract and support, even in a small space.

40 FEED THE BIRDS

Bird feeding is a popular activity already, probably because of the extra benefits of seeing birds visiting your garden. In the UK, 15,000 tonnes of peanuts are put out for birds every year, and in America, bird-feeders and seeds are a billion-pound industry.

The best way to attract a wide range of birds to your garden is to provide a variety of different foods:

- Peanuts are favourites with a wide range of small birds, as well as starlings.
- Sunflower seeds help provide a balanced diet, and are best bought without shells.
- Nyjer seeds are the favourite food of goldfinches. They are very tiny black seeds, and can be bought from pet shops or online bird-food specialists. They are easily spilled by feeding birds, so a feeder with a tray is best for these seeds.
- Seed mixes are also available, containing a suitable range of seeds for garden birds.
- Special 'fat cakes', containing seeds and insects embedded in energy-rich fat, are great for attracting blackcaps.
- Live mealworms are a fantastic treat for birds during the breeding season, although handling them isn't for the faint-hearted.
- Never put out salted peanuts, crisps or other salty foods, as they will dehydrate the birds, which can be fatal.

A traditional bird table is suitable for most gardens, although models with a roof are better, as this will keep your garden birds safer from predators, such as sparrowhawks.

Help prevent squirrels and cats climbing up by fixing an inverted plastic bottle or metal tin over the post, underneath the tabletop. Position the table within range of a hedge to give the birds a handy escape route from predators.

Hanging feeders are excellent, as they can be positioned away from potential threats and in view of your house. You can find a wide range of feeders in the shops, including many squirrel-proof models. A stick-on window feeder provides an incredible close-up view of your winged visitors.

Supplement your feeding by planting bird-friendly plants. Soft fruits and brambles are ideal, and ivy, rowan and holly all provide attractive berries. Plants with seeds that birds will enjoy include thistles, teasels, poppies, sunflowers and honeysuckle.

Bird baths

Creating a bird bath is another golden opportunity to reuse old materials in the garden. Almost anything that can hold water can be used, although bright colours should be avoided and the bath shouldn't be too slippery. A layer of gravel will help.

Place your bird bath in a shady spot away from places that cats could use as an ambush point, and raise it up off the ground. Traditional bird baths with pedestals work well, so mimic this design if you can.

Bird boxes

The house sparrow – as its name suggests – likes to nest around houses. However, both houses and gardens are becoming less and less bird-friendly. Providing a secure nesting place is a great way to look after your local bird population.

Sparrow box (also suitable for tits and other small birds):

Place the box out of direct sun, between two and four metres from the ground. Place it close to the eaves of a house, or attach it to a tree using wire or a fixing band.

MAKE FRIENDS WITH INSECTS

Many friendly insects, such as bees and butterflies, like to eat or lay their eggs on one particular species of plant. Encourage insects by providing these favourites in your garden:

- Buddleia (the 'butterfly bush')
- Nettles (where butterflies lay their eggs)
- Lavender (a bee magnet)
- Honeysuckle (with lots of nectar)
- Cat mint (although this also attracts cats, as its name suggests)

Other beneficial insects need places to hibernate over the winter, and you can buy specialist insect homes for aphid-eating species, such as lacewings and ladybirds. Ladybirds like to hibernate in dead wood, so a simple bunch of twigs pushed into a plastic tube can be an effective home, too.

Attach your insect hideaway to a tree, windowsill or shed in a sheltered spot. Position it where it won't collect rain and make sure it can't be blown down by strong winds or otherwise disturbed.

42 CREATE A BOG OR POND

You can create a small pond in even the tiniest garden and still do a great job of encouraging wildlife.

It's amazing how good nature is at exploiting the tiniest ecological niche. When I was about ten years old, I buried an old baby bath in my little corner of the garden and filled it up, hoping to raise some frogs. The tadpoles I hatched did fine for a while, but then a huge mayfly nymph appeared and started attacking them. I have to confess I was far too impressed at having an exotic visitor in my pond to be very upset about my tadpoles losing their limbs!

You'll want to do a more professional job than I did with your pond, and there are lots of guides that will go through pond care step-by-step. Here are a few brief tips to get you thinking:

• To protect visiting animals, put it near cover, such as bushes or a rockery, but away from trees.
• Make sure it has shallow edges as well as a deeper section to stop it freezing. Float a ball in the pond in winter to keep part of the surface unfrozen.
• Fill the pond with rainwater, taken from your water butt.
• Don't put in goldfish as they will eat some of the wildlife that comes to live in the pond. And don't take animals from other ponds either. Newts, frogs and toads – as well as mayflies – will soon find it for themselves.
• Don't use garden chemicals or wood treatments near your pond (though this is not a problem if you are using organic methods).

A BOG GARDEN

You can create a bog garden next to your pond, or have a bog instead of a pond if you have small children.

Animals, such as frogs and toads, and a wide range of insects, will appreciate an area of marshy ground. In some areas, you may even attract grass snakes – don't worry, they are harmless (and protected by law!)

• Build a bog in a similar way to a pond, but dig a much shallower hole before lining it.
• Put in a layer of soil, then fill it up with rainwater before planting up.
• There are some beautiful plants that will like your bog garden and attract insects. Marsh marigold, yellow flag iris and snake's head fritillary will all do well and look great.

43 PLANT A HEDGE

Hedges provide many things essential for wildlife, including shelter, food, protection from predators and a corridor between habitats. Hedgerows are found in both urban and rural areas, but most are under threat: in the countryside from herbicides used on nearby crops, and because they are removed to create larger fields; in towns they are cut down to make way for new buildings, or just because they have been neglected and look untidy.

I grew up on a 1970s housing estate built on farmland, and we were lucky enough to be left with a short stretch of original hedgerow along the bottom of our garden. It mainly consisted of hawthorn, along with some old tree stumps that supported some glorious fungi (and one year attracted a huge nest of wasps). The hedge brought a wide range of birds to the garden and we enjoyed watching two or three families nesting in the hedge every year.

Planting a hedge

It is important to put native species in your hedge. Hawthorn, holly, beech and yew are all ideal, and the pricklier species will also provide a barrier to burglars. Privet is perfect for nesting sparrows, but needs regular trimming to stay in good shape. A privet hedge in flower is terrible for triggering hayfever, so either prune your privet well or avoid it altogether if you have allergies.

For a good hedge, buy small trees and bushes from a number of species and plant them out in autumn in a stepped pattern (or ideally a double row) for a good width. Put shade-loving wild plants, such as wood anemones and violets, at the bottom of your hedge to create a good starter eco-system for all the new wildlife.

Hedges are not difficult to look after. Simply make sure you keep chemicals away from them and then trim them into shape every autumn, so they don't become full-grown trees.

And if you haven't got room for a hedge, growing ivy up a wall can help wildlife, too. Bees will be attracted to the flowers and birds will eat the tiny fruits. If it gets thick enough, small birds will even nest in it.

44 CREATE A WILD CORNER

A wild corner of the garden, where you don't dig or disturb things, can be a wonderful haven for birds, insects and small mammals. Depending on whether you are in the town or country, you could also end up providing shelter for larger mammals, such as foxes or even badgers.

An already-neglected spot behind a shed or next to the compost bin is ideal for a wild area. You could put in native plants, such as rose bay willowherb, which is the weed with lovely pink flowers you often see along railway tracks, or just leave the grasses, nettles and brambles to flourish and let it develop from there.

Add a range of useful items to your wild corner, such as old wood to encourage fungi, or rocks, under which mice, voles and toads can burrow.

ORGANIC GARDENING

On a full-scale farm, organic practices have many benefits, including better soil, good yields with fewer chemicals, more wildlife and more jobs for farm workers. The hidden environmental costs of organic farming are only one third of those from farming with industrial methods.

Many of these benefits can also be brought into your own garden. In particular, your efforts to attract wildlife and support local birds will work all the better if you garden as organically as you can.

Not using chemical fertilisers and pesticides makes it very important to feed your soil with good compost – not a problem if you are also reducing waste by filling up a compost bin. And healthy plants will naturally be more resistant to diseases and pests.

The six basic principles of organic gardening are:
1. Feed the soil, not the plants.
2. Grow resistant and native varieties.
3. Practise crop rotation.
4. Do companion planting.
5. Encourage predators.
6. Use physical barriers and traps.

The first three of these principles have already been covered in previous chapters because they are the basics for any good garden – not just organic ones. Healthy soil is a much more robust foundation for successful gardening than feeding individual plants with artificial fertilisers, and almost every organic gardener uses crop rotation to preserve soil fertility.

The other three principles are covered in more detail from here. 'Be vigilant' is the final tip. When it comes to pests, prevention is better than cure so take a walk around your garden every few days and keep an eye out for any problems. Often, simply removing and destroying leaves and branches where insects or other parasites have taken up residence will remove the problem.

45 COMPANION PLANTING

Planting together species that deter each other's pests is a great way to reduce the need for pesticides. Adding colourful flowers to your vegetable plot makes it look attractive, too – there's no reason why a kitchen garden can't be beautiful as well as useful.

Good companions include:
• Marigolds with tomatoes, to ward off greenfly and blackfly and attract aphid-eating hoverflies.
• Dill with any plant that is a target for aphids, as it attracts hoverflies.
• Carrots with leeks. These vegetables repel each other's pests.
• Chives with sunflowers and tomatoes, as they have a strong onion scent, which annoys aphids.
• Californian poppies around a vegetable patch will attract ladybirds and hoverflies.
• Tansy, with its strong smell, is disliked by ants.
• Nasturtiums with cabbages, as a decoy for caterpillars. Nasturtiums have lovely orange and red flowers, which can also be eaten in salads.

ENCOURAGING PREDATORS 46

All your efforts to make your garden wildlife-friendly will bring benefits to your organic vegetable garden, as the species you attract will prey on many common garden pests.

Who eats what:
• Hedgehogs have a huge appetite for slugs and snails.
• Toads and centipedes will also help keep your slug population down.
• Lacewings and ladybirds are fantastic aphid-hunters.

If you develop a pest problem, you can even buy predatory species and parasites from mail order firms and release them into your garden. Some of these organic controls work in rather grim ways, such as the parasitic wasps that lay their eggs inside whitefly larvae and consume them from the inside, or the tiny nematode worms that burrow into the backs of slugs and infect them with bacteria.

47 BARRIERS & TRAPS

Other preventative measures involve stopping pests from reaching your plants by putting physical barriers in the way, or by luring them into traps.

• Prevent weeds by laying mulch, bark or gravel around your plants. Any that do grow up through the mulch can be more easily spotted and pulled out.

• Use fine-mesh netting to protect cabbages from butterflies or to protect young seedlings from a range of flying insects. Unfortunately (as I have discovered), if you have a cat, he may find the netting an irresistible plaything.

• Single plants can be protected with mini-cloches made from old plastic bottles cut in half – push them about 10cm into the soil for an effective barrier to slugs.

• A trap for whitefly can be made from a piece of board painted yellow and then coated with liquid soap (or eco-friendly washing-up liquid). Leave it out near your cabbages and it will soon become covered in whitefly. Wipe it off and recoat to trap more.

Slugs and snails
These are the pests that I have had most trouble with in my efforts at urban gardening. Sometimes, when I have lost whole plants overnight, it even seems as if they have launched an organised attack.

If you have a plague of local snails and slugs (and while you wait for helpful predators to colonise your garden), I'd recommend showing no mercy and trying all these tips at once:

• Any barrier around your plant that has sharp edges will deter them. Sharp gravel spread around the vegetable patch, or even broken egg shells on the surface of a pot, should help.

• Grease spread around the top edges of pots can also stop them getting in, although it needs renewing quite often.

• Copper tape can be bought from garden centres to be attached in a band around pots and frames (my friend puts this around her bookcase strawberry frame – see page 89). The copper gives the slugs an electric shock when they try to crawl over it, but it must be kept clean.

• Bran, sprinkled around the vegetables, can cause slugs and snails to dehydrate when they eat it.

• Beer traps really work, and leave a feast of non-toxic drowned slugs for local predators. Simply bury a jam jar level with the ground and half-fill it with beer, and the slugs will dive in happily.

SAVING WATER
IN THE GARDEN

Water used outside the home is responsible for 7 per cent of the total amount of tap water consumed by the average household. But at peak times in summer, this can rise to more than half.

Gorgeous, productive, relaxing gardens don't have to waste clean drinking water on a grand scale. Careful use of supplies, collecting rainwater and using grey water from the shower or washing-up can help reduce what you take from the taps, and you can cut the amount your garden needs with clever planting as well.

Follow these water conservation tips for a greener garden, in more ways than one.

48 DRIER GARDENING

Plant more drought-resistant varieties in your borders. Shrubs with woody stalks will put up with dry weather well. Other plants to try including are:

- Buddleia
- Alyssum
- Catmint
- Rosemary
- Thyme
- Hardy geraniums
- Spurge (euphorbia)
- Baby root vegetables
- Peas
- Spinach

Use mulch around your plants to help the soil retain moisture in the sun. Leafmould is ideal for this, as is fibrous compost or gravel. Apply mulch after rain or watering when the soil is already moist.

Don't worry about having a brown lawn in summer. It will take more water than the world can spare to keep it really green, and it will recover quickly anyway after the drought. Don't cut your lawn too short and it will hold moisture better.

If you are growing crops in pots, these can need watering a lot. Put water-hungry crops in grow-bags, as these help retain water better.

USE WATER WISELY 49

Always use a watering can rather than a hose. Hoses can use up a hundred litres of water in a few minutes, and sprinklers can be even worse.

If you have a very large garden, use a hose attached to your water butt and invest in a trigger nozzle, so that you can turn off the flow between plants.

Target the water at the base of the plants not the leaves. For large, spreading shrubs and trees, the best place to water is above the ends of their roots (roughly where the ends of their branches reach to) rather than next to the trunk.

Time your watering carefully. Early in the morning or in the evening is best, so the water can soak right into the soil before the sun evaporates it.

50 ALTERNATIVES TO TAP WATER

Your plants actually prefer rainwater. Grey water from the house can also be used in the garden to make more savings.

Collecting rainwater

A water butt attached to the downpipe from your guttering can help to capture some of the tens of thousands of litres of water that fall onto your roof every year.

Fitting a water butt is relatively simple, and several can be joined together to catch even more water. You can get standard water butts to hold between 100 and 300 litres of rainwater from garden centres, and these are usually made from recycled plastic. Smaller sizes are also available for patios.

Make sure your water butt has a lid that children can't remove, and prevent it becoming a home for breeding insects by floating polystyrene balls or chips on the surface of the water – another great way to use up unnecessary packaging! Place your water butt on a stand to make sure there is room beneath the tap for your watering can.

If you are gardening on a balcony or a small roof terrace that can't take the weight of a full water butt, you can still capture small amounts of rainwater by leaving out upright watering cans.

Grey water

Grey water is water from the house that has been used for washing. Even with soap residues, it is safe to use for watering the garden. However, avoid using it on vegetable and fruit crops, just to be on the safe side.

Grey water should be used straightaway rather than stored, so never put it in your water butt.

Collect grey water by showering with a bucket nearby to catch the drips, or you can buy an adaptor kit for your hosepipe to turn it into a siphon for bringing water from a bath into the garden.

Soapy washing-up water is ideal for cleaning up a path. Remove any food scraps and pour it onto the stones before sweeping away the dirt. Of course, this is better for your garden if you are using biodegradable washing-up liquid made from plant extracts.

FURTHER INFORMATION & ADVICE

 ## BEING GREENER IN THE HOUSE

Heating and cooling
The Energy Saving Trust has advice on energy saving and links to available sources of grants to help with insulation.
www.energysavingtrust.org.uk

Warm Front provides grants to pensioners and people on benefits to insulate their homes.
www.warmfront.co.uk

The HEAT project website provides a clear and simple guide to grants and support for home energy-saving and insulation.
www.heatproject.co.uk

The National Insulation Association has lots of information on how to improve the heat-retention ability of your home.
www.nationalinsulationassociation.org.uk

The Sustainable Building Association has factsheets covering a range of eco-building and maintenance issues.
www.aecb.net

George Marshall of the Climate Outreach and Information Network has been turning an ordinary terraced house in Oxford into a DIY eco-home for several years. Read the story and get loads of useful information from his website.
www.theyellowhouse.org.uk

Saving electricity

The Energy Saving Trust has advice on reducing electricity wastage.
www.energysavingtrust.org.uk

The National Energy Foundation has advice on saving electricity.
www.nef.org.uk

The Carbon Trust helps businesses reduce their impact on the climate.
www.carbontrust.co.uk

Green electricity

The Centre for Alternative Technology in Wales has a wealth of
advice on energy saving and green electricity.
www.cat.org.uk

The Renewable Energy Centre provides information on the
different green energy technologies.
www.therenewableenergycentre.co.uk

The Green Energy Works website from the Green Party shows
examples of green electricity being generated today.
www.greenenergyworks.org.uk

The National Consumer Council produces reports abouts topics
such as food miles and green electricity tariffs.
www.ncc.org.uk

The Low Carbon Buildings Programme administers national
government grants for green energy projects in the UK.
www.lowcarbonbuildings.org.uk

The British Wind Energy Association promotes and monitors the
development of wind energy.
www.bwea.com

Solar Century supplies solar panels and has case studies of projects.
www.solarcentury.com

Saving energy in the kitchen

The Energy Saving Trust has a guide to energy-saving appliances and an up-to-date list of recommended products and suppliers.
www.energysavingtrust.org.uk

The Women's Institute has launched a carbon challenge, and provide lots of simple tips for being greener everywhere in the home, not just the kitchen.
www.womens-institute.co.uk

Be a clever eater

Farmers Weekly has lots of information about food miles and benefits of buying local food on its campaign website.
www.fwi.co.uk/gr/foodmiles/index.html

Find your local farmers' markets at:
www.farmersmarkets.net

Sustain is an organisation that promotes fairer and greener farming, and which produces 'food facts' reports about a range of environmental issues.
www.sustainweb.org

The Soil Association certifies organic food for the UK and has lots of information about the benefits of going organic in the kitchen on its Why Organic website.
www.whyorganic.org

The Women's Institute's Carbon Challenge has lots of information about food sources, storage and waste.
www.womens-institute.co.uk

Vegetarianism

The Vegetarian Society provides lots of tips to help you eat less meat, as well as a host of good recipes.
www.vegsoc.org

The BBC Food's recipe archive has many excellent vegetarian and vegan recipes.
www.bbc.co.uk/food

The 8th Day Co-op Café in Manchester has collected together its favourite vegetarian dishes.
www.eighth-day.co.uk

The Savvy Vegetarian website has some great ideas for kid-friendly vegetarian meals.
www.savvyvegetarian.com

Saving water in the home

The Waterwise website is a fantastic online resource for water-saving tips.
www.waterwise.org.uk

The Environment Agency is part of the UK government and has lots of information about conserving water resources.
www.environment-agency.gov.uk

The Water Guide is a hub for information about the UK water industry, with advice for consumers on where our water comes from, as well as tips for saving water.
www.water-guide.org.uk

Reuse and recycle

RecycleNow has recycling information for the home, garden, workplaces, schools and other situations. Interesting facts as well as some good tips.
www.recyclenow.org.uk

The Waste & Resources Action Programme aims to improve how we use resources and reduce waste, and campaigns to reduce packaging as well as increase composting and recycling.
www.wrap.org.uk

WasteOnline has factsheets on numerous topics surrounding waste and recycling, with tips on recycling everything from car tyres to computers.
www.wasteonline.org.uk

The Recycled Products Guide has a searchable database of products made from recycled materials.
www.recycledproducts.org.uk

Get info on where to find the best vintage, recycled and ethical clothes, as well as details of greener food and beauty products on the Style Will Save Us website.
www.stylewillsaveus.com

Be a greener cleaner

Ecover products are biodegradable and are even made in green factories in Belgium and France. They are available in many shops and supermarkets.
www.ecover.com

Look in health food shops for other eco-friendly cleaners. They will stock a wider range than most supermarkets, and also check out the online retailers on page 127.

Greener DIY

The Green Building Store has eco-friendly building products and articles giving detailed advice on many of the topics covered in this chapter.
www.greenbuildingstore.co.uk

The Association of Environment Conscious Building has useful links and information about greener buildings and materials.
www.aecb.net

The Forest Stewardship Council certifies sustainable timber and has a searchable product database to help you find supplies.
www.fsc-uk.org

The Eco-Renovation Network has a business directory as well as case studies and blogs, and even organises co-operative buying of eco-friendly materials.
www.eco-renovation.org

The Home Improvements Sustainability Guide website has been produced by the Scottish Building Standards Agency and has lots of useful advice.
www.sbsa.gov.uk/homeimprovements.html

BEING GREENER IN THE GARDEN

Gardening advice

There are so many places to find advice on growing flowers, fruit and vegetables in the garden. These organisations have good information on environmentally friendly and organic gardening.

Garden Organic – from the Henry Doubleday Research Association
www.gardenorganic.org.uk

Royal Horticultural Society
www.rhs.org.uk

BBC Gardening online
www.bbc.co.uk/gardening

Helping wildlife in the garden

The RSPB has a wildlife gardening guide that will help bring birds back into your garden.
www.rspb.org.uk

Wild About Gardens from The Wildlife Trusts has the answer to almost every question about local wildlife and your garden.
www.wildaboutgardens.org

The Space for Nature wildlife gardening resource encourages gardeners to aim for maximum biodiversity.
www.wildlife-gardening.org.uk

Saving water in the garden

The Waterwise website has water-saving tips for the garden, as well as the home.
www.waterwise.org.uk

The Royal Horticultural Society has downloadable reports on many aspects of water conservation.
www.rhs.org.uk

The Sunshine Garden website has ideas for creating urban gardens that aren't thirsty.
www.london.gov.uk/sunshinegarden

Eco-friendly products

Greener products for the home and garden can be hard to find on the high street. Mail-order shopping can provide the answer, so use your search engine to shop around, or try these online shops to find a range of products more easily.

Centre for Alternative Technology shop
www.cat.org.uk/shopping

WWF's Earthly Goods shop has a wide range of eco-friendly products.
www.wwf.org.uk/shop

Nigel's Eco Store
www.nigelsecostore.com

Natural Collection
www.naturalcollection.com

Green Gardener
www.greengardener.co.uk

Ethical Consumer magazine rates a wide range of products on different ethical criteria. Their website has sample guides available for free to non-subscribers. www.ethiscore.org